"EYES AN
Insect Life

By
Arabella B. Buckley

NEW WEST PRESS

Copyright © 2023 by New West Press

ISBN 978-1-64965-026-9

All rights reserved. This book or any portion thereof may not be reproduced or used in any manner whatsoever without the express written permission of the publisher except for the use of brief quotations in a book review or scholarly journal.

Ordering Information:
Special discounts are available on quantity purchases by corporations, associations, educators, and others. For details, contact the publisher at the listed address below.

U.S. trade bookstores and wholesalers: Please contact New West Press:

email: contact@nwwst.com

PREFACE.

These books are intended to interest children in country life. They are written in the simplest language, so as to be fit for each class to read aloud. But the information given in them requires explanation and illustration by the teacher. I have, in fact, tried to make each lesson the groundwork for oral teaching, in the course of which the children should be encouraged to observe, to bring in specimens, and to ask questions. Then when the chapter is read and re-read, as is the case with most school books, it will become part of the child's own knowledge.

No one can be more aware than I am how very slight these outlines arc, and how much more might have been given if space permitted. But I hope that much is suggested, and a teacher who loves nature will fill in the gaps.

The charming illustrations will enable the children to identify the animals and plants mentioned.

ARABELLA B. BUCKLEY

EYES AND NO EYES SERIES.

By Arabella B. Buckley.
With Numerous Illustrations.

Book I.   Wild Life in the Woods and Fields.
Book II. By Pond and River.
Book III. Plant Life in Field and Garden.
Book IV. Birds of the Air.
Book V.   Trees and Shrubs.
Book VI. Insect Life.

CONTENTS.

I. What is an Insect?...1

II. Parts of a Caterpillar. 5

III. Familiar Moths. 9

IV. Familiar Butterflies. 15

V. Injurious Beetles. 20

VI. Useful Beetles. 25

VII. Wasps and their Ways. 30

VIII. Solitary Bees. 36

IX. Hive Bees. 41

X. The Two-Winged Flies. 46

XI. Crickets and Grasshoppers. 52

XII. Ants and their Honey-Cows. 57

"EYES AND NO EYES"

Sixth Book.

INSECT LIFE.

LESSON I.

WHAT IS AN INSECT?

It is a lovely summer morning. Let us shut up our books and wander in the garden and field, in search of insects. The best way is to take a few card match-boxes with us, and drop one insect into each as we find them. Then when we get back to school, we can put them separately under tumblers.

Insects are so small that we often pass them by. But they form three-fourths of the whole animal kingdom, and they do us so much good and so much harm that we ought to know about them.

As we start I see a Cabbage Butterfly in the kitchen garden, and a beautiful Red Admiral flitting about among the flowers. We will take the Cabbage Butterfly, so that she may not lay her eggs on our cabbages.

Next stop at this rose-tree, there are a number of tiny insects, on the flower-stalks. If you look closely, you will see that each one has his beak buried in the stem, so as to suck out the juice. These are plant-lice. Each one is called an Aphis, and in the plural they are called Aphides.

We must syringe the tree with soft soap and tobacco water, or it will soon be covered with these insects, for they increase at the rate of more than a million in a month, and they stick out all the sweet sap from the plants to which they cling. On the same tree you will very likely find a Lady-bird, for she feeds on aphides.

Now look into the flower of this old Cabbage Rose, which grows in most cottage gardens. You are almost sure to find in it a lovely Rose-beetle with green shining wings shot with gold. Take it up and look at the bright wing-cases. While you are looking, it may open these cases and spread out the transparent wings underneath; but if it flies away you can easily get another.

Now, look! At your feet runs a beetle which is not half so pretty. It is the Cocktail, or Rove Beetle, often called the Devil's Coach-horse. As you pick him up he will cock up his tail and squirt out a very disagreeable fluid over your fingers, while he raises his head and snaps with his jaws. So drop him in his box quickly. The fact, is, he is terribly frightened, and hopes to make you set him free.

Now we will go out into the newly-mown field, and there you will see a number of small green Grasshoppers hopping about. They have been hatched under the earth-clods, and are eating the tips of the young grass. Some will have wings, but others, which are not fully grown, will have none. Pick one up and make him too a prisoner.

Next try to find a Wasp or a Bee. You can pick it up in your handkerchief and drop it in its box. We must go down to the river to find a May-fly or a Dragon-fly, and near there we shall easily get a Daddy-long-legs. But if there is not one to be seen,

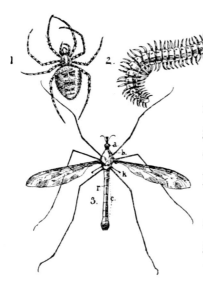

1. SPIDER. 2. CENTIPEDE
3. DADDY-LONG-LEGS.
k. Knobs or balancers.

a Blue-bottle or a Gnat will do.

You will wonder that I have not asked for a Spider. You had better get one, and also a Hundred-legs or Centipede, if you can find it.

When you have put these specimens under their glasses, look carefully at them. You will find a difference between the spider, the hundred-legs and all the others. The spider has eight legs and the centipede a very great many, while all the others have only six.

Now look at the Grasshopper, the Wasp, and the Daddy-long-legs. You will see very clearly that their bodies are divided into three parts—(a) the head; (b) the front body, on which the six legs and the wings grow; (c) the hind body, which has no legs on it, even when it is very long, as in the daddy-long-legs and the May-fly. You cannot see these divisions quite so well in the beetle because its wing-cases cover the join between the front and hind body.

We had better call these three divisions by their right names—(a) head; (b) front body, or, thorax; (c) hind body, or, abdomen. It is because insects are cut into these three parts that they have their name. It comes from the Latin "inseco" (I cut into). The Spider's head is not clearly divided from its

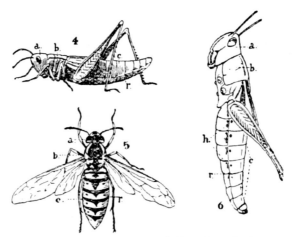

4&6. GRASSHOPPERS. *h*. Breathing holes.
5. WASP. *r*. Rings. *a*. Head. *b*. Thorax
c. Abdomen.

body, and a Centipede has not three divisions. For this reason, and because they have not six legs, some naturalists separate them from the true insects. This is why I did not call them insects.

Another thing you can notice well in the little green Grasshopper: his body is divided into rings (r), from his tail up to his head; and you can see the same in the wasp and the daddy-long-legs, the aphis and the cocktail beetle. All insects have ringed bodies.

It is these rings which enable the Wasp to bend her abdomen (c) when she wants to sting and to breathe. You can see, as she stands, how it keeps moving up and down all the time. This is because she is breathing. How do you think she does it? Not through her mouth as we do, but through her sides.

If you look closely at the grasshopper you will see along the sides of his body, some little black dots, one in each ring. These are breathing holes, and through them the air goes in and out.

They are smaller in a wasp, but they are there, and she is pumping the air in and out of there.

Now that we have put aside the spider and the centipede, those that remain are true insects. But there is a difference between the daddy-long-legs and the rest, which you must notice. This is that they all have four wings and he has only two. This would be very strange if it were not that we can find some remains of the right number. He has two little knobs (k) behind his front wings, and with these he balances himself. So he has two wings and the stumps of two more.

There is a great deal more to be learnt about these insects. But I want you to remember now that they have six legs; that their body is divided into three parts: that you can see the rings in their hind body or abdomen; that their legs and wings grow on the front body or thorax; and that they never breathe through their mouths. Also that while bees, butterflies, and beetles have four wings, flies have two wings and two stumps.

Find as many insects as you can, and notice their different parts.

LESSON II.
PARTS OF A CATERPILLAR.

IN the last lesson we found the full-grown insects very easily. But it is often more difficult to know some of them when they are young. Grasshoppers, crickets, and plant-lice, when they come out of the egg, are very much the same as when they are grown up, except that they have no wings. But the daddy-long-legs begins its life as a grub underground. The lady-bird when young is a kind of caterpillar and runs over the plants eating plant-lice. And beetles are grubs with six small legs before they grow into perfect beetles with wings.

The caterpillars of Moths and Butterflies are easy to find, so we will look at one in this lesson. There is hardly any time in the summer that you cannot find a caterpillar. Those of the Orange-tipped Butterfly come out first in April. In May the Cabbage Butterfly lays her eggs, and soon the caterpillars are eating the young cabbage leaves. A little later you may find among the nettles the black caterpillars with white spots which will turn in June into the Peacock Butterfly; or the dark green caterpillars of the Red Admiral. These are hidden in a bunch of leaves generally tied up with caterpillar silk.

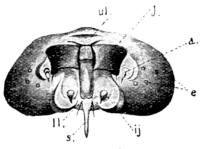

CATERPILLAR'S HEAD.

ul. Upper Lip. *j*. Jaws. *a*. Antennae.
e. Small Eyes. *ij*. Inner Jaws.
ll. Lower Lip. *s*. Spinning Tube.

If you do not find either of these you cannot miss the heaps of little black caterpillars striped with yellow which feed under the leaves of nettles, and turn into the small Tortoiseshell Butterfly. These caterpillars are very useful in killing nettles, so the butterfly is one you should always be glad to see. Then towards the autumn the caterpillars of the big Hawk-moths do a great deal of mischief. If you go out in the evening or early morning you may find the caterpillar of the Spurge Hawk-moth feeding on the green spurge in the hedges. It is a fine creature three inches long, with three bright lines on its back, and yellow spots on each ring.

But the most common one, which I have often found, is

the caterpillar of the Privet Hawk-moth, which feeds in the evening on the privet hedge or the lilac bushes. It is from three to four inches long, and is a bright apple-green, with seven sloping violet stripes on its sides, and a horn at the end of its body. Its head is green, edged with black, and the breathing holes on its sides are circled with bright orange.

It destroys the hedges terribly, for it is very hungry and wants to store up food so that it may grow into a moth. Though its body is soft, its head is hard and horny, and as its mouth has nothing to do in breathing, or making any noise, it can be used all the time for eating. It is made of a great many pieces, but the parts you can see well are the large upper lip ($u\ l$) and the two broad strong outer jaws (j) which move to and fro sideways as it gnaws the leaf. As soon as a piece is cut off the caterpillar tucks it into his inner jaws ($i\ j$), where it is chewed and swallowed. Under the jaws is the flat lower lip ($l\ l$), through which passes a little tube. Look well at this tube (s). It is the place from which comes the silk, which he uses to spin his cocoon, in which he sleeps while his butterfly body is growing.

You remember we read in Book I. that the spider spins her web out of silk which comes from six little pockets under her body. But a caterpillar or a silkworm brings its silk out of its mouth.

Now look at the legs. There are three pairs, one on each ring of the thorax. They have joints in them and claws at the end. These are true legs, and they are hard and horny like the head. When the caterpillar turns into a moth these six legs will remain. But it has also some cushion feet, on the other rings of its body, which it uses to hold fast to the twigs. These are not true legs, but only fleshy cushions with a ring of hooks under them, and they will disappear with the caterpillar's body when the moth grows up. There are generally four pairs of cushion feet behind the true legs, and two pairs at the end of the body, but some caterpillars do not have so many. Do you know those called "Loopers," which bend their body into an arch or loop? You may often find them on the currant bushes, where they do a great deal of mischief. They have only six true legs and four cushion feet at the end of their body, and they walk in a curious fashion. They hold firmly to the twig by their front legs, and then draw up their cushion feet till their body makes a loop in the air. Then they let go with their front legs and lift up their head like an elephant raises his trunk, and stretch forward further up the twig.

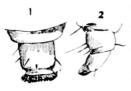

1. CUSHION FEET OF CATERPILLAR.
2. JOINTED LEGS.

As a caterpillar is always eating, his skin becomes so full that there comes a time when he cannot put in any more food. Then he remains quiet for a few hours, and swells out his rings. His skin splits and he creeps out, with a new soft skin ready underneath. This will stretch, and very soon he is eating away as merrily as ever.

He does this about five times in his caterpillar life, and then he stops eating and remains without moving for some days. His colour fades, and when he splits his skin and shuffles it off, all the parts of the butterfly or moth are to be seen underneath, soft and unfinished. Soon a kind of gum oozes out over them. This hardens and keeps the tender body safe from harm while it is growing.

Now he is called a *chrysalis*, or sometimes a *pupa* or doll;

and, indeed, he looks like a crumpled doll as you see his legs bent together and his head folded down over them under the hard gum. The pupa of a butterfly is generally broad at the top and narrow at the bottom, and it has ridges and prickles on it. But the pupas of moths are shaped more like an egg, and are smooth. Moths generally wrap their pupa in a silk bag or cocoon, but butterflies leave theirs naked, and fasten it to a stem or a blade of grass with a silken cord.

The caterpillar of the Hawk-moth works its way down into the ground and lies in a hole which it lines with silk. I had one in a large flower-pot once for many months. After about seven months, or sometimes much longer, the pupa wriggles up to the top of the ground, and then breaks through its cover and comes out as a moth.

Bring in some caterpillars, each with the plant on which you find it. Keep them fed and watch their changes.

LESSON III.
FAMILIAR MOTHS.

WHEN Moths creep out of their cases they no longer do us any harm. They spread their wings and fly about sipping honey from the flowers. Their strong jaws have almost disappeared, and feathery lips take their place. Their inner jaws have grown very long, and are rolled together into a long double tube—very like a tiny elephant's trunk. When the insect is not using this trunk it is rolled up under its lip, but when it wants to reach the honey in the flowers it unrolls the trunk and thrusts it into the blossoms.

In the early morning, or evening in August, you may see the

1. PRIVET HAWK MOTH. 2. CATERPILLAR. 3. CHRYSALIS.
4. TIGER MOTH. 5. CLEARWING MOTH.

Privet Hawk-moth with its beautiful rose-coloured wings striped with black, thrusting its head into the honeysuckle in the hedge. Or the large brown Humming-bird moth may be hovering in the sunshine over a bed of flowers in the garden, or sucking honey out of the deep flowers of the evening primrose. You may know it partly by the humming noise it makes with its wings, and partly because it does not settle on the flowers, but sucks as it flies.

Then there is the Death's-head Hawk-moth, which is the largest moth in England, and has this curious name because the grey marks on the back of its thorax are something like a skull. It has brown front wings, and yellow hind wings, with dark bands across them, and its feelers and trunk are very short. You may find it, if you look out after sunset in the autumn, fluttering over the hedge, for it is not nearly so rare as people think, only it always flies by night.

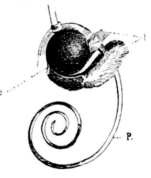

HEAD OF A MOTH.
e. Large Eye. *l*. Lips.
p. Proboscis or Trunk.

If you get one of these big moths you will be surprised to see how different it is from the caterpillar out of which it grows. The six legs are still there on the three rings of the thorax, but there are four splendid wings above them. These wings are made of very fine transparent skin, and are covered all over with scales, which are arranged like tiles on a roof. However carefully you take hold of a moth or a butterfly you will always find some fine dust left on your fingers. Each grain of this dust is a lovely scale, and it is these which give the moth its beautiful colours. Moths and butterflies are called Lepidoptera, because this word means "scale-winged." The caterpillar had six small eyes, so tiny that we did not notice them. The moth has these still, but it has besides two glorious globes on each side of its head, cut into hundreds of little windows, so that the moth can look every way, although the eyes do not move. The eyes of the Death's-head moth shine like red lamps in the dark night.

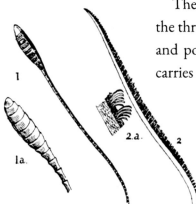

1, 1a. ANTENNAE OF BUTTERFLIES.
2. ANTENNAE OF THE PRIVET HAW-MOTH WITH PLUMES AND SCALES (2a)

The moth is plainly divided into the three parts. Its hind body is oval and pointed, its broad front body carries its legs and wings, and its head carries the big eyes (e), the delicate feelers, and the sucking trunk. The feelers or antennæ of moths are broad in the middle and pointed at the end, and they have tiny feathers on them. By this you may know moths from butterflies. For the antennæ of butterflies are nearly always round and thick at the ends like a club and have no feathers on them.

Another difference between them is, that butterflies fold their wings upwards over their backs so that the upper side of the wings touch each other, while moths lay theirs down on their backs like a roof on a house.

One common moth you may find is the Goat-moth. It has a short body and brownish white wings with wavy black lines on them. You will find it resting on the leaves of the willow or poplar. It does not fly about much, for it has no trunk, and does not eat any food during its short moth life. It only wants to find a place on which to lay its eggs, which will hatch into a naked red grub. This grub will bore its way into the tree and live there for years, eating the wood.

Many moth grubs live inside trunks and branches. If you look over the currant bushes on a hot summer's day you will often find a pretty little moth with a narrow yellow and black

SIX-SPOT BURNET MOTH WITH IT'S CATERPILLAR AND COCOON.

body, thin legs, long feelers and clear transparent wings, very unlike most moths. This is one of the Clearwing-moths, which have scales round the edge of their wings only. It is so lazy that you will easily catch it, and it looks so like a gnat that it is called the Gnat Clearwing. This moth lays its eggs in the twigs of the currant bushes, and its little yellow caterpillar, with a black line on its back, eats its way into the pith of the twigs. You should always clear away the dead or faded twigs on the currant bushes, for fear these caterpillars should be in them.

Another moth which you may find flying in the bright sunshine is of a dark blue-green colour, with six bright crimson spots on its wings. It is the Six-spot Burnet-moth, whose cocoons you may find in May fastened on the blades of long grass in the meadow. By August the moth is out and flits from flower to flower.

There is one more moth which you will like to know, because its caterpillar is the Woolly Bear, or Hairy Man, which curls itself up in a ball when you pick it up. It is very fond of feeding on the lettuces and strawberries, and when it is ready to change it bites off its long hairs and weaves them into its cocoon. When the moth comes out it runs about the flower beds in the evening and does not fly very high. But everyone knows it as the Tiger-moth, for it is the grandest moth we have. Its front wings are cream coloured with wavy brown stripes on them. The hind ones are bright scarlet spotted with black. Its thorax has a bright red band on it, and its abdomen is scarlet with black bars. If you can find a Woolly Bear in the early summer and keep it in a box with a piece of wire over it and give it plenty of dead nettles to eat you may see its cocoon and the grand Tiger-moth which comes out of it.

Try to find a Hawk-moth, a Clearwing-moth, a Tiger-moth, and the cocoon of the Burnet-moth. Bring in caterpillars and cocoons, when you can find them, always with a piece of the plant on which they feed.

LESSON IV.
FAMILIAR BUTTERFLIES.

THERE are not nearly so many butterflies as there are moths. But as the moths often fly at night, we know butterflies best, because they flutter about in the bright sunshine. Their caterpillars do not do so much harm in the garden as the moth caterpillars, except those of the Cabbage butterfly, which we read about in Book III.

You will find it very interesting, in the spring and early summer, to look for the chrysalis of each common butterfly, and keep them in a box with a piece of coarse muslin over it, so as to watch when they come out.

If you do this you will see their colours much better than by catching them, because when they first come out of their sheath, their wings are not battered with wind and rain. And you need not kill them, when you have looked at them you can set them free to enjoy the sunshine.

It is curious that so many butterflies lay their eggs on the leaves of stinging nettles. Perhaps it is because the cows and sheep will not eat these plants, so the eggs are safe. The Peacock butterfly, the small Tortoiseshell, and the Red Admiral all leave their eggs on nettles. It is there that you will find their pupas or chrysalises. Let me tell you how to know them.

The eggs of the Peacock butterfly are gummed in patches under the nettle leaves, and in June you may find the little black caterpillars spotted with white all feeding together in groups. Early in July they will each of them have spun a little cushion of silk under some leaf, by which the curious stiff

BUTTERFLIES.

1. PEACOCK BUTTERFLY ON WING. 1a. AT REST. 2. CATERPILLAR.
3. CHRYSALIS. 4. BRIMSTONE BUTTERFLY. 5. CHRYSALIS.
6. ORANGE-TIP BUTTERFLY. 7. CHRYSALIS. 8. FEMALE AT REST.
9. SMALL HEATH BUTTERFLY. 10. AT REST.

chrysalis hangs head downwards, looking like a brown shining shell.

If you carry home either the caterpillar (2), or the chrysalis, you will find that about the end of July a glorious butterfly (1) will come out. Its hind wings are brown and its front wings bright red and blue, and on each of the four wings there is a large bright eye-spot, like the eyes on a peacock's tail. The body is dark blue, and the feelers on the head are long and thin, with knobs at the end. But when the butterfly shuts its wings (1a), all the bright colours are hidden and the whole insect is brown like the trunk of a tree, with pale edges like wood newly cut, so that the birds are not so likely to see it when it is resting.

But, if you bring home another chrysalis from the nettles by mistake, a different butterfly will surprise you. This one has wings much notched round the edge, and they are coloured black with red markings and white spots. It is the Red Admiral, whose pupa also hangs head downwards under nettle leaves. You will not make this mistake if you find the caterpillar, for it is not black like that of the Peacock butterfly, but dark green with a yellow line on its sides, and it has spikes all over it. It feeds on nettle leaves which it ties round itself with silken threads. And you must remember that these green and yellow caterpillars will turn into Red Admirals.

Again, you may find a bunch of nettle leaves tied together with silk, which have many caterpillars inside them. These will be very spiny, and have four yellow stripes on their black bodies. They will turn into small Tortoiseshell butterflies.

Unless you know these three kinds of caterpillars well, the safe way is to bring them all home and keep them till the butterflies come out, and then notice many little differences which I cannot give you here.

On the thistles you may find another caterpillar which draws the leaves round it, and whose chrysalis has gold spots upon it. This will turn into a reddish brown butterfly called the Painted Lady. In some years there are very few of these, while in other years they are plentiful.

Our next search shall be among the alder trees by the riverside either in the early spring or about the end of July, for there are two broods of this butterfly.

You must look among the small twigs for a pretty green chrysalis with red dots on it, something like a ribbed shell. It will be tied round the middle to the stem of the twig by a fine rope of silk. Notice how cleverly the caterpillar has swung it, so that the heavy broad end balances the long thin one. Then cut off the twig and take it home. The chrysalis will turn into the Brimstone butterfly (4), whose pale yellow wings have four red spots on them. You will

1. TORTOISESHELL BUTTERFLY.
2. AT REST.
3. CHRYSALIS.

know it quite well, for it is generally the first butterfly to come out in the spring.

Next we shall have to look low down among the plants by the roadside. There are some with white and pink flowers whose petals are in the form of a cross. They are called rock-cress and bittercress, and if you can find out which they are, and look under their leaves you may find a most curious chrysalis shaped like a boat pointed at both ends. This will turn into the Orange-tip butterfly (6), which has a broad orange patch on the tip of its front wings. This butterfly is very gay when it is flying, but when it settles (8) and folds its wings upwards, it can scarcely be seen on the flowers of the wild parsley from which it sips honey. This is because the underside of the wings are dotted with green and like the tiny parsley flowers with their white petals and green centres.

Another common butterfly is the small Heath (9) which may be seen any fine day in June or September sipping honey from the heath on the common. It feeds as a green caterpillar on the tall grasses, and comes out a pretty little butterfly with tawny yellow wings, with a round eye-spot.

Now you know how to look for caterpillars, and chrysalises, and butterflies, you can learn about them for yourself. Anywhere on the violet beds you may find the spiny caterpillars of the pretty striped and dotted butterflies called Fritillaries. Blue butterflies are found mostly in chalk districts, though the Common Blue lives almost everywhere, and you may often see the little Copper butterflies flying with it, their dark glittering wings gleaming amongst the lovely blues. And wherever you see a butterfly on the wing you should try to follow it till it alights, for one of the most interesting points to notice, among all butterflies, is how the under colour of their wings helps to hide them when they are resting, while the upper colour is bright and gay.

Bring in caterpillars and chrysalises, and watch them. Notice the plant on which the caterpillar feeds. Compare the under surface of their wings with the plants on which they settle.

LESSON V.
INJURIOUS BEETLES.

ALL living creatures must hunt for food, and insects eat a great deal for their size. Beetles are very heavy feeders. They eat most when they are grubs, but some, like Cockchafers and Tiger-beetles, eat almost as much when they are full-grown and have their wings.

There are plant-eating beetles, and beetles which feed on other insects and animals. Altogether there are more than 3,000 species of beetles in the British Isles. It is useful to know what kind of food a beetle eats, for some do good work in the fields and gardens, while others do great injury to the crops.

One of the most mischievous is the Cockchafer. You know him quite well when he flies in your face in the evening. But perhaps you do not know him as a grub, when he lives for three or four years underground, and eats the roots of the grass, corn, and vegetables. If you see plants in the cornfield or garden looking sickly and yellow, and drooping their leaves although the ground is damp, it is most likely that there is a grub underneath, and it may be the grub of a Cockchafer.

Dig up the plant and you will find an ugly white creature

like a huge maggot, almost as thick as your little finger, with a red head and very strong jaws. It has six long legs, with five joints, growing on the rings behind its head, and is so full of food that it can hardly crawl. The end of its tail is swollen into a thick cushion, and you can see the breathing all along its sides very clearly because it is so distended with food. You remember that it does not take in breath through its mouth, so it can go on eating all the time. If you had not disturbed it, it would have crept on from plant to plant across the field, doing nothing but eat for three years. It goes down deeper in the ground in winter to keep warm during the frosty weather.

At last in the autumn of the third year it draws itself together, and leaves off eating for nearly eight months. If you can find one at this time you will be able to see the parts of the real beetle crumpled up under the clear skin, and for the last few months it will be a full-grown sleeping cockchafer.

Then, when the warm summer comes, it crawls up above ground and flies into the trees, eating their leaves as greedily as it ate their roots while it was a grub. This is the time to catch and kill them, for they only live about a month, and meanwhile the mother cockchafer lays the eggs which will hatch into grubs.

You will be surprised to see how different the beetle is from the white grub you found underground. It is now a flying insect, about half an inch long, with brown powdery wing-cases, covering a pair of transparent wings. Its hind-body, or abdomen, ends in a fine point, and on its head it carries a pair of feelers tipped with broad folds like a half-open fan.

These folds are very handsome in the male Chafer, but much smaller in the female (2), and by this you may know the

DESTRUCTIVE BEETLES.
1. Male Cockchafer. 2. Female. 3. Grub.
4. Pupa. 5. Cock-Beetle or Skipjack.

mother which will lay the eggs. You must catch and kill these last if you want to save your crops, and the most merciful way to do this is to drop them into boiling water. A crushed beetle is a long time dying, but boiling water kills them at once.

You will find that they rest in the daytime on favourite trees, and, if you spread a cloth underneath, you may beat the boughs and so catch a good many. Farmers use gas-lime and other dressings to kill the grubs in the ground.

Another very mischievous creature is the young of the Skip-jack or Click-beetle. All children know these little beetles, though perhaps you may not know their name. They are narrow and flat, about half an inch long, with very short legs. The most common one in England has reddish wing-cases, striped with long furrows, and a black head and thorax. Boys love to pick them up, and turn them on their backs, for they bend themselves up in the middle so as to rest on their head and tail. Then with a sudden jerk and a click they straighten themselves, so that their back hits your hand and sends them up in the air, and they come down the right way up. Sometimes they fall again on their backs, then they rest a little and begin again.

These amusing little creatures are very destructive when they are grubs, for the wireworms we know so well are the young of the Click-beetle. If you find a wireworm and look at it carefully you will see that it is not a worm, but has the six legs on the rings behind its head, by which you know that it is an insect. Wireworms feed on the roots of most plants. They are long and narrow like a piece of wire, and are generally of a reddish yellow colour, and have very tough skins.

The Click-beetle lays her eggs in meadows, and among the roots of plants, and the wireworm when it is hatched often feeds for five years before turning into a beetle. Therefore Click-beetles must be destroyed, and salt and lime sprinkled on the earth to kill the grubs.

Unfortunately the pretty little Weevil-beetles are also very destructive. We read in Book I. about the Nut-weevil, and almost every plant and tree has some weevil which attacks it. There is the weevil of the apple-blossom (4), the Pea-weevil (1 and 2), the Bean-weevil (3), the Furze-weevil, the Vine-weevil, and many others. They all begin life as little soft maggots with no true legs, but only cushion feet, and with horny heads and sharp jaws.

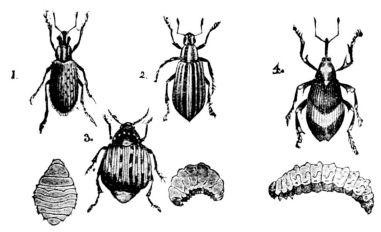

1. SPOTTED PEA-WEEVIL. 2. STRIPED PEA-WEEVIL.
3. BEAN WEEVIL. 4. APPLE-BLOSSOM WEEVIL

You may know the full-grown weevils by their prominent snouts, sometimes broad and sometimes long. They are beautiful little creatures with polished wings which shine like jewels, and bright eyes; but as grubs they destroy the flowers, fruits, and green shoots everywhere.

Some of the most curious are the Stem-boring weevils. They have long snouts and very sharp jaws, and their feet have hairy pads underneath with sharp hooks at the end, so that they can cling firmly to smooth stems. If you search on the poplar tree in summer you may find a lovely Stem-borer with shining green wings and red eyes; and on the fruit trees of the orchard you are almost sure to find the Steel-blue weevil which lays her eggs in their shoots.

When the mother stem-borer wants to lay, she bores a hole in a young shoot with her snout and forces an egg into it. When she has laid several in this way, she sets to work to cut off the shoot with her sharp jaws. This often takes her some weeks, and if you see the hanging shoot and burn it you will destroy the grubs. But at last, when it hangs by only a thread of bark, she weighs it down, and it falls to the ground, where the grub feeds in peace when it is hatched.

Try to find Cockchafers—male, female, and grub. Bring in a Click-beetle and a Wireworm. Find as many weevils as you can; and twigs, flowers, and fruit with grubs in them.

LESSON VI.
USEFUL BEETLES.

We cannot help destroying some beetles when there are so many that they eat our crops. But it is pleasant to know that there are others which do us so much good that we need not wage war upon them.

The Tiger-beetles, for example, are very hungry creatures; but, as they feed on other insects, they destroy the weevil and cockchafer grubs, wireworms and caterpillars, and so save our plants. Their name is given to them because they are so fierce and cunning. They are not very large—our common tiger-beetle is not more than three-quarters of an inch in length—but their long slender legs are very strong, and they can fly very fast.

There are always plenty running about in the hot sun across dry, dusty fields or commons in summer. Their wing-cases are a beautiful shining green colour shot with copper, and dotted with five yellow spots. They run very gracefully, and so fast that you will find it difficult to catch one. Just as you think you have it, it will suddenly open its wing-cases, spread its delicate transparent wings, and be off almost before you can see it go.

But if you can catch it, you will see that it has large eyes standing out on each side of its head and two sharp jagged jaws for tearing its prey, while the lower ones are covered with stiff bristles which help to hold it.

And now you must look for its grub, which is a very curious creature. The best way to find it is to go to some soft part of a sandy field where you have seen the Tiger-beetles running about. Then look at any small holes in the sand, and try to find one which leads to a tunnel in the ground. The grub of the Tiger-beetle sits at the mouth of this tunnel to catch insects as they pass. It will disappear as soon as you come near, but if you put a blade of grass into the hole and shake it, the grub will grasp the blade, and you can pull it out.

Then you can see the tools it uses. It is a long soft white grub with a horny head, and jaws like sickles, and, besides its six brown spiny feet, it has two soft humps on its back with little hooks on them. As soon as this grub is hatched in the ground, it scoops a tunnel in the soft sand with its spiny legs, and pulls itself up to the top, holding on by its legs and the hooks on its back. Its head just fills the hole, and as it is a poor weakly creature and cannot move fast, it keeps quiet till some

USEFUL BEETLES.
1. Tiger Beetle. 2. Cocktail Beetle. 3. Sexton Beetle burying a Mouse.

insect passes, and then darts its head out and pulls its victim down. If you have the patience to find some of these tunnels, and sit still and watch, you may see the grub catch its prey.

The Rove or Cocktail-beetles, which we found in the first lesson, are very useful in eating insects, though they are not beautiful. But the Ground-beetles, which have only small wings under their wing cases, and seldom fly, are the best hunters. You may sometimes see a good-sized beetle with long legs running along through the grass. Its body is very dark, shaded with red and violet. This is the Violet Ground-beetle, and it is hunting for grubs and wireworms.

There are some very curious beetles not difficult to find which will interest you. These are the Sexton, or Burying-beetles. When you see a dead mouse or bird lying in some part of the field or garden, pick it up quietly. If it has been there a few days it will already have a bad smell, and you are almost sure to find underneath it two or more beetles with thick bodies and strong legs. They are generally black with red feelers, and two light red bands on their abdomen. These are Sexton-beetles, which have scented the dead body and flown, often for some distance, to bury it.

They scrape away the soft ground underneath, till the body sinks down, and then they drag the earth over it. Why do you think they do this? Because the mother beetle wants to lay her eggs there that the grubs may feed on the flesh. She does this as soon as the animal is buried, and in a few days the grubs are hatched. They are narrow, and each has six legs and a number of spines along its back. With these it wriggles through the flesh, and eats away till it buries itself in the ground and turns into a beetle.

INSECT LIFE.

A great many beetles are useful to us by eating dead and living animals. Among these are the little black shining Mimic-beetles, which draw up their legs and pretend to be dead when they are touched, and the Glow-worms, which shine so brightly in the lanes in the summer nights.

A good gardener who sees a glow-worm in a hedge will always pick it up gently, and put it in his garden when he has the chance. For the young of the glow-worm is a soft grub, which works its way into the shells of small snails and feeds upon them.

If you find a dry snail-shell with a white grub in it, it will most likely be the grub of the glow-worm. You may know it by a tuft of white threads on its tail, which it uses to brush off the slime of the snail from its back.

When they are full-grown you will find the mother glow-worm (1) very easily at night, because she gives out such a bright light. She has no wings, and you might take her for a slug if you did not notice her six little legs. The male glow-worm (2) has two spots of light near his tail. But he is not so bright as the female. He has long soft wing-cases and broad wings, with which he often flies into a lighted room when the window is left open.

The last useful beetle we can mention is the little Ladybird. She feeds all her life long on the plant bugs and aphides which destroy our plants. Wherever there are plant-lice, there the ladybird lays a bunch of yellow eggs and, when they are hatched, the long dark grubs clamber up the plant stalks and poke the lice into their mouths with their front feet. After a time each one glues its tail to a leaf and hangs till it becomes a ladybird,

GLOW WORMS.
1. Female with glowing light.   2. Male with faint light.   3. Grub.

and then it flies away to feed on plant-lice on some other bush and to lay more eggs.

Bring in a Tiger-beetle, and try to find its grub. Search for Sexton-beetles under dead animals. Bring in a Mimic-beetle. Find a male and female glow-worm. Look for the grub of the Ladybird.

LESSON VII.

WASPS AND THEIR WAYS.

We all like Butterflies because they are pretty, and Bees because they give us honey. But no one likes Wasps, for we are always afraid that they will sting, and they spoil our garden fruit. Yet wasps are very industrious and interesting. They act as scavengers, eating offal, raw meat, and insects, and they never sting unless they are frightened. You may be stung by pressing a wasp without knowing it. But people are very silly who flap them, and keep dodging about when they are near, for if you sit quite still they will not hurt you.

We are obliged to kill wasps, or we should be overrun by them and have no fruit, and the best way is to keep a good look out in the spring and early summer. The few big ones which come out then are queen wasps, or mothers, and each one will found a nest. It is more merciful to kill these, than to have to take nests in the summer, when there may be as many as 3,000 or 4,000 in each. Most boys have seen a wasps' nest dug out at night, but perhaps you have never looked at one carefully. Let us see how it is made.

When the queen-wasp comes out from under the moss or grass, where she has spent the winter, she looks out for a hole in the ground, left perhaps by a mouse or a mole. Creeping into it, she makes it larger by biting the earth and kicking it out with her hind feet. Then she flies away and scrapes small pieces of fibre off the trees and plants. You may sometimes see her scraping window frames or posts with her jaws. She is getting shreds of wood. With these she goes back to the hole, and works them up, with some gluey matter from her mouth, into a kind of greyish paper or cardboard.

Before it hardens she plasters this into the top of the hole, making a thick lump, which she glues to the roots of plants. Then she starts afresh for more fibre, and with it builds a few cells under the lump.

She lays an egg in each, and then goes on making more paper and more cells. In about eight days the first eggs are hatched into legless grubs, and she feeds them with honey and insects, still going on with her work. In about three weeks the grubs spin their cocoons, and in another week they come out as working wasps. After that, some come out almost every day, and the queen-wasp leaves them to do the work of building the nest and feeding the grubs, while she only lays eggs.

INSIDE OF COMMON WASPS' NEST.

They not only build cells, they also cover the nest with a papery dome of several layers, which hangs like an open umbrella, from the lump at the top. When they have finished one comb it is like a round plate, and is smooth above, with a great number of cells underneath, all opening downwards.

The wasps then make several gluey pillars under this comb to hold up a new one below which they form in the same way as the first. So they go on till August, when there may be fifteen or sixteen flat round plates one below the other, joined by a number of pillars. Then they draw the papery dome in at the bottom so that the whole nest is a round or oval-shaped ball. As wasps do not store honey, these combs are only cells for grubs. The papery covering prevents the wet soaking in from the bank.

In August they build larger cells, out of which come males or drones which have longer antenna; than the workers and queen-wasps. These queens are larger than either the males or workers. They soon fly out of the nest and pair with the drones

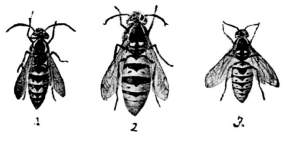

1. MALE.   2. QUEEN WASP.   3. WORKER.

and as winter comes on the wasps kill any grubs which remain, and, growing sleepy and dull, die themselves, leaving only the queen-wasps to sleep till next spring. Then if you know where there is an old nest you can dig it carefully out and see the long tunnel in the bank, along which the wasps went in, so that no one might know where their nest was.

Some wasps build under the roofs of houses, especially the large wasps called Hornets, unless they choose the old trunk of a tree. If you look in a wood you may sometimes find the nest of the Wood-wasp hanging under the bough of a tree, though you would scarcely notice it unless you follow a Wood-wasp home. They are built like the other nests, only they have a thick papery column down the middle.

Besides the common wasps there are a great many smaller kinds, some of which you may find. They are very interesting, because they carry insects into a hole and bury them with their eggs, so that the young grub may have food when it is hatched.

There is a pretty little wasp, generally called the Wall-wasp, which you may see in June or July biting the mortar in the garden wall or making holes in a sandy bank. It is smaller and blacker than the common wasp, and has a few bright yellow bands on its hind body. It scoops out a tunnel in the mortar and leaves the pieces sticking round the hole. Then after going in to see that all is right it comes out and flies away, coming back presently with a small green caterpillar. It carries this in and goes off for another, and so it goes on till it has brought about fifteen or twenty.

If you dig out the mortar along the wall, so as to open this tunnel, you will find at the end an egg hanging by a thread. The wasp put the egg there before she went for the first caterpillar. Between this egg and the hole the fifteen little caterpillars will be lying curled up one beyond the other. The curious thing is that they are not dead. The wasp has only stupefied them with her stings so that they do not try to escape. If you do not break into the nest she will stop the hole up with the pieces of mortar round the edge and leave it. Then when the grub has eaten the caterpillars and turned into a wasp it will bite its way out.

Then you may find some of the Sand-wasps, which dig so many holes in the sandbanks on heaths, or in the lanes and gardens, wherever it is sunny and warm. One of these, called the

SOLITARY WASPS.
1. Wall Wasp.   2. Sand Wasp.

Hairy Sand-wasp, puts Spiders in her hole for the grub to eat. She is orange coloured, with a black head and straggling legs. But she is very strong and can drag a big spider to her den.

I have not room to tell you more of these curious wasps, some of which fill their nests with beetles, others with crickets. But now you know about them you will follow any you see and watch their habits for yourself, which is much the best way.

Find an old wasps' nest and try to make a drawing of it. Notice the shape of the common wasp and compare it with any others you find. Notice particularly the difference in the thread joining the abdomen to the thorax.

LESSON VIII.
SOLITARY BEES.

We all know the Hive-bee well, but perhaps you have not noticed that there are other kinds of bees flying in the garden. Some of these are about the same size as the hive-bee; some are much smaller, and they are differently marked.

Most of these are solitary bees. There are no neuters among them, only males and females living in pairs. Others live in great numbers in the holes of sandy banks, but do not work together.

If you have ivy growing on your cottage, you must often have noticed small bees flitting in and out of the flower. Among these there will most likely be one, about half an inch long, with a black body covered with a tawny down. She will have two little horns on her head, and is called the "Two-horned Osmia".

If you can watch one and follow her, you may see her fly into some old rotten post, or tree-stump. Then if you cut into the post near the hole you will find a curious nest. For this bee bores a long tunnel and builds a waxen cell at the bottom. Here she lays an egg and puts round it bee-bread, made of pollen and honey from the flowers. She has no groove in her leg like the hive-bee, so she carries the sticky pollen in the thick hairs under her body, and scrapes it off with a comb on her feet.

When she has laid the egg and put in food, she seals the cell with wax, and begins another on the top of it. So she goes on till she has filled the tunnel.

But how is the bottom bee to get out? Her egg was laid first and she has eight or ten others on the top of her. Strange to say they wait for each other. They all become perfect bees about the same time, and, if one below is ready sooner than the others, she eats through the cover of her cell and tries to push past her neighbour. But if the one above is so big that the bee cannot get by without hurting her, she waits patiently till all are ready.

Another little bee which you may often find is the Sleeper bee, so-called because she often sleeps in the blossoms of flowers, where you may find her. She is thin and black with a square head and strong jaws, and she has a little yellow down on her hind body or abdomen. She too burrows in posts, but very often she makes her nest inside a large straw. In olden days, when cottages were thatched, hundreds of these bees would build in the larger straws of the thatch, and might be heard buzzing about the roof.

Then there is another bee which you cannot help finding.

SOLITARY BEES.

1. Osmia Bees. 2. Sleeper Bee.
3. Leaf-Cutting Bee. 4. Carder Bee.

This is the Leaf-cutting bee. Have you not seen the leaves of rose-trees with pieces like a half-moon cut out of their edge? If you watch you may see a bee doing this work.

She is about the same size as a hive-bee, but rather stouter, and her body is black with soft brown hairs over it. She clings to the leaf and turns round in a circle biting as she goes. Just before she has finished she opens her wings and so balances herself in the air. Then, when the last bite is made, she flies off with the piece of leaf carried between her feet and her jaws.

She goes to a hole in the ground, which is straight down for a little way, and then turns, and runs along under the surface. Here she packs the leaf in and goes back for more. With several pieces she makes a

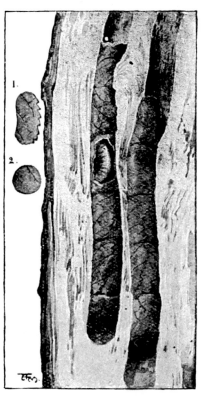

NEST OF LEAF-CUTTING BEE IN A TREE.

One Cell cut open showing the Grub.
1. Leaf cut for the Sides.
2. Leaf cut for Bottom of each Thimble.

little thimble, in which she lays an egg, with food round it, and closes it with three or four round pieces. Then she begins another thimble, pushing it in, so that it fits a little way into the last one. In this way she builds about seven cells, each with its egg and bee-bread, for the grubs to feed on till they turn into bees. Though you will easily see the bees cutting the leaves, you will not so easily find their tunnels, for they fill in the earth again at the top, so that the entrance cannot be seen. The best way is to follow a bee which has been cutting a leaf, but she is so quick you will have to be quick too. Sometimes she makes her hole in a willow tree when the wood is soft.

NEST OF THE BRAMBLE OSMIA, WITH A YOUNG OSMIA SHOWN IN A CELL.

There is another Osmia which makes its nest in the stem of the bramble. It hollows out the pith and covers the cells with it. When you see a blackberry stalk with the end bitten off, you may as well cut down a little way with your knife and see if there is a tunnel in it, with bee-cells, or wasp-cells, inside.

Another very curious bee, called the Carder bee, lines its tunnel with fluffy hairs and cotton stripped off plants. You will remember that the ragged robin and wild campion have their stems covered with thick down. The "Carder bees" strip this fluff off the plants, roll it up in a ball, and fly away with it to their nests in the ground, where they use it to make their cells.

Solitary bees do not store honey for the winter like the hive bees. They die off in the autumn, all except some mothers, which creep into holes and sleep till the spring, when they make their nests and lay their eggs.

There are so many of them that I cannot tell you about them all. You must watch for yourselves, and you will soon learn to notice the little holes in the trees and the ground, and in some of them you are sure to find curious creatures.

Notice different kinds of solitary bees, and try to find their tunnels in the spring.

LESSON IX.

HIVE BEES.

HIVE bees are so much at home in our gardens, that I am afraid most people think they know all about them, and take very little notice of them. This is unfortunate, because bee-keeping is very interesting, and many more cottagers might make money by bees, and at the same time become really fond of these busy little insects.

When all the bees in the hive had to be killed each time the honeycombs were taken, we could not get fond of our bees. But now, even cottagers can have boxes and glasses on the top of their hives so as to take the combs without destroying the little friends who fill them for us.

The hive-bee is a wonderful insect. She has three pairs of legs, and two pairs of wings just like a Wasp. But the hind pair of legs is longer than the others, and she has a groove in each of them which makes a kind of basket, into which she packs pollen from the flowers, and carries it home to make bee-bread for her grubs. You may often see a bee going into a hive with both its hind legs heavily laden with sticky pollen. It is puzzling at first to guess how she gets it into the basket, but, if you look lower down her leg, you will see that it is covered with hairs which form a small brush. When she comes out of a flower her hairy body is covered with pollen-dust, and she brushes it off with one leg, making it into a little lump, which she packs into the basket of the other leg.

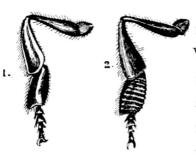

HIND LEGS OF BEE.
1. Outer Side.
2. Inner Side with groove for Honey.

Her mouth is a most useful tool for getting honey. When she is not sucking, her trunk is drawn in under her strong jaws. But when she is feeling for honey, this trunk, which is really a long under lip with a hairy tongue inside it, is thrust into the flower and brings back the honey, which she passes down her throat into a honey-bag, or first stomach.

Then she flies back to the hive. There other bees take the pollen out of her basket as she goes in, and she passes on to the cells, and pours into them the honey from her throat. Some of this honey is used to feed the young bee-grubs, and the rest to fill the honey-combs for the winter.

Sometimes, however, the bee does not pour out the honey, but goes to the top of the hive, and hangs quietly by her front feet. After about four and twenty hours the honey is digested in her stomach, and part of it forms bees-wax, which oozes out under her body into eight little pockets. Then she goes down into the hive, and licks this wax out with her strong jaws, moistens it with her tongue into a kind of paste, and uses it to build the cells of the comb.

It is when the bees are out getting honey and pollen that they are so useful to the gardener. You will remember that the vegetable marrows cannot grow unless the bees carry pollen from one flower to another. Our plants have better flowers and our fruit trees bear better fruit because the bees fly to and fro and carry pollen from one to another.

But if the bee carried it haphazard from one kind of flower to another it would be of very little use, for strange pollen would not make the seeds grow. Watch a bee and you will find that she very seldom visits more than one kind of flower on the same journey. She will fly from one bed of violets to another, or from apple-tree to apple-tree. But she will not in one journey go from an apple-tree to a pear-tree, nor from a violet to a primrose. We do not know why she does this, but it is very useful to us, and all gardeners should encourage bees in their garden.

BEE HAGING AND SHOWING THE WAX-POCKETS UNDER HER BODY.

And now, if you want to keep bees, you must learn a few simple things. You must always be very gentle and quiet with them. They will soon learn to know you, and to understand that you are not afraid of them.

If you have a straw hive it should measure about sixteen to eighteen inches across, be about eight or nine inches high, and flat on the top, with a hole in it in which a plug is fixed. Put this hive in a warm sheltered part of the garden on a wooden bench about fifteen inches from the ground. Then in May buy a swarm of bees which has just come out from a neighbour's hive. Smear your own hive inside with balm and sugar, and hold it under the bough on which the swarm hangs. Shake the bough gently till the bees fall in. Turn the hive down on to a piece of wood, and in the evening carry it gently to your garden. The next morning the bees will be busily at work. The big heavy drones will wander about idly, but the smaller working bees will go out and collect honey, hang up in the hive till they have wax in their pockets, and begin to build the comb. If your swarm was the first to leave the hive, the old queen bee, which was in the middle, will soon begin to lay eggs in the cells—about 200 a day. But a second swarm is led by a young queen, and she will fly out with the drones before she settles down in the hive. Now the working bees will be very busy. In two or three days the first eggs are hatched, and the nursing bees feed the grubs with honey and pollen which the other bees bring in. In about five or six days they seal up the

BEE-HIVE WITH WOODEN SECTIONS ON THE TOP AND GLASS WINDOWS IN THE SIDE.

mouth of each cell, and the bee-grub spins its silken cocoon, in which it turns into a bee in ten days more. Then it comes out and works with the rest.

The empty cell will soon be filled with honey; but it will be brown, not white and clean like the "virgin" honey which is put into new cells. After about six weeks the queen lays some eggs in larger cells, out of which come males or drones. Then about every three days she lays an egg in a cell like a thimble, on the edge of the comb. The grub in this is fed with special food, and becomes a queen-bee.

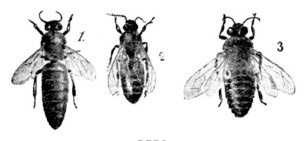

BEES.
1. Queen.   2. Worker.   3. Drone.

Unless you have a hive with a glass window in it you cannot see all this going on. But about the beginning of June you may expect that the hive is getting full of combs and bees. Then is the time to take out the plug at the top, and put on a bell-glass, or a box of wooden sections. In these the bees will make comb which you can take away. You must put in a small piece of comb to tempt the bees to build, and then you must put a straw cover or some old cloths over the whole to keep it warm and dry and dark.

In about a month you will find this upper hive full of honey-comb sealed up in the cells. You can take it off with a cloth dipped in weak Condy's Fluid, for the bees do not like this, and they will not come near you. These sections of honey-comb will be pure and clear, and you can take them away without killing a single bee.

In July you may get one or more new swarms, and then when September comes you must take off the top and cork up the hive for the winter. But remember that you have taken a great part of the bees' store of food and you must feed them with honey and sugar during the cold weather.

Examine three bees—male, female and neuter. Examine trunk and hind legs of the working bee. Get a piece of brown honey-comb with remains of bee-bread and young bees. Compare it with pure honey-comb. Watch a bee among the flowers. Find honey-comb with thimble cells on the edge.

LESSON X.
THE TWO-WINGED FLIES.

THERE are a number of small flying insects which belong to the same family as the Bees and Wasps, such as the Saw-flies, which destroy our vegetables, and the Gall-flies which make those curious galls we found on the oak-tree and other trees. But though we call these "flies" you may always know them from true flies because they have four wings, while all real flies have only two.

Try to collect as many two-winged flies as you can. There will be the common House-fly, the Blue-bottle or Blow-fly, Gnats, Midges, Daddy-long-legs, Horse-flies, and many others.

The House-fly and the Blue-bottle are both very useful in their right place, for they eat decaying matter and dead animals. But they do great harm if we allow them to multiply in the wrong place.

If you have a great number of flies in your house you may be sure that there is dirt somewhere, for the House-fly lays her eggs in dung heaps, dust-heaps, or on any dirt she can find behind a shutter or door, or in an unswept corner.

She lays about 150 at a time, and in a day or two the little legless grubs are hatched, and feed on the dirt. In four or five days they leave off eating and rest in their grub-skin, which grows hard and brown. Then in summer they come out as full-grown flies in about a week. But in winter the hard pupa often lies for months, and people who do not clean their house thoroughly in autumn are likely to have a plague of flies next year.

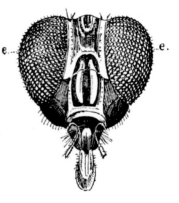

HEAD OF BLOW-FLY SHOWING THE LARGE COMPOUND EYES.

The Blue-bottle or Blow-fly lays her eggs *(a)* on meat of any kind, or on the bodies of decaying animals. When her grubs are hatched they are very useful in ridding us of bad-smelling creatures, for they give out a kind of liquid which makes the flesh decay more quickly so that they may eat it.

All boys know "gentils" *(b)* used for fishing. These are the maggots of the Blue-bottle, and when they have done feeding they grow soft inside and draw themselves up into an egg-shape. Then they give out a liquid which hardens their skin

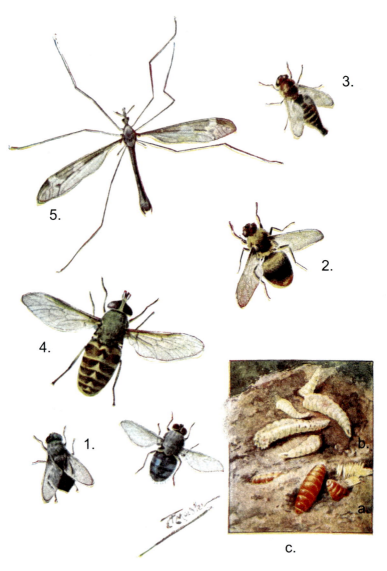

FLIES.
1. Blow-Flies.   2. Oxbot Or Warble Fly.   *a*. Eggs.
b. Maggot.   *c*. Pupa.   3. Horse Bot-Fly.   4. Gad-Fly.
5. Daddy-Long-Legs.

into a shiny reddish brown case *(c)*. Inside this the Blue-bottle forms, and then pushes its head out between two little lids at the top of the cocoon.

If you catch a Blue-bottle and put it under a bell-glass with a few grains of sugar you may watch it put out its trunk and feed. You will see that it turns and twists the sugar as if it were playing with it. But all the time it is wetting it with some liquid which it sends down its trunk so as to work the hard lump into syrup which it can suck up. If you press the thorax of a Blue-bottle very gently with your finger and thumb it will put out its trunk and you can see the thick lips at the end with the sucker (A) between them. But you will want a magnifying glass or a microscope to see a little lancet (l) which it has inside its trunk, and which it uses to pierce the skins of fruits, when it wants to suck their juice.

There are two kinds of flies which are much more hurtful than the common fly or the blue-bottle. These are the Gad-flies and the Bot-flies. You know one of the small Gad-flies quite well, for it drops on our hands, or our neck, when we are sitting out of doors, and lets us know that it is there, by giving a sharp bite to suck our blood. We call it the Horse-fly because it teases the horses so much in summer; but there are many others we do not know so well. The largest English Gad-fly is about an inch long.

TRUNK OF BLOW-FLY WITH THICK LIPS.
A. Sucker.
l. Lancet.

The Bot-flies are more dangerous than the Gad-flies, for instead of biting with their mouths they prick with a sharp tube at the end of their abdomen, so as to lay their eggs under the skin of an animal. The Bot-fly or Warble-fly of the ox looks very like a humble bee, only she has two wings instead of four. She has a pointed tube at the end of her body, with which she pricks the skin of the ox, and lays her eggs underneath it. In a short time the eggs hatch, and the maggot irritates the flesh so much that large lumps are seen on the side or back of the animal. If the farmer does not press out the maggots from these lumps, and put a proper dressing on them, the beef of the ox will be poor and bad, and no feeding will make it any better. When the maggot is full-grown it drops to the ground to make its change.

The horse Bot-fly does not put her eggs under the skin, but sticks them, with a little slime from her mouth, to the hairs of the horse on his shoulder or under the knee.

When the egg is ready to break, the warmth of the horse's tongue, as he licks himself, makes it crack and the grub slips down the horse's throat to his stomach. There it feeds, and when it is full-grown passes out with the dung.

The way to check this grub is to keep the skin of the horse clean and the hair short. This Bot-fly is rather larger than the House-fly, with bright yellow markings and a very hairy body.

I wonder how many grubs you know of those gnat-like flies, with thin feelers and legs, which fly in the fields and over the rivers. We read about the gnat in Book II., but you should know the midges, which attack wheat and other grain.

The Wheat-midge is a little orange yellow fly, about the size of a very small gnat. Early on a June morning, when the wheat is in flower, you may shake these midges off the stalks and see them flying near the ground. The mothers have a sharp tube as thin as a hair, with which they lay their eggs in the wheat blossom. There they hatch into little red maggots, which feed on the grain and often destroy half a crop.

You ought to know, too, the grubs of the Daddy-long-legs, which do so much harm to our crops. If you see a Daddy-long-legs clinging to a blade of grass she is most likely thrusting her egg-tube into the ground to lay her eggs.

These hatch into legless brown grubs with strong jaws and a pair of short horns. Farmers call them "Leather Jackets," and you may find them when you are ploughing damp fields. Or you may find the hard pupa, which is shaped like a Daddy-long-legs with its wings folded, its legs drawn up, and two horns on its head. It has spines on its abdomen, with which it will drag itself up when the fly wants to come out.

The best way to get rid of these hurtful grubs is to plough the ground deeply and bury the eggs or maggots, so that they die, or cannot get to the surface, or to put a dressing of gas-lime or other insect-killer on the land. Starlings are very useful in pulling them out of the ground and eating them.

Find grub and pupa of Blue-bottle. Examine a Blue-bottle—legs, body, and proboscis. Try to find House-fly eggs. Bring in a Horse-fly. Try to find the Bot-flies of the ox and the horse. Find a Wheat-midge and its grub; also the grub and pupa of the Daddy-long-legs.

LESSON XI.
CRICKETS AND GRASSHOPPERS.

ALL the insects about which we have been reading are different when they are young from what they are when full grown. But young Crickets and Grasshoppers when they come out of the egg are much the same as when they are older, except that they are smaller and have no wings. They jump and eat and behave in the same way as their parents, and change their coats four or five times. After the last change you can see their wing-cases under the skin, and, when this bursts, they spread their wings and fly.

If you make a cage of wire gauze and put some young crickets in it, and feed them with damp leaves, you may see these changes. But do not try with a muslin cover, as a friend of mine did. For crickets have strong jaws and soon eat their way through.

The little green Grasshoppers of the fields are easy to find, but the large green Grasshopper, is not so common. Still if you know where to look, in the nut-hedges and woods, you may often catch one, and it is a fine insect to examine. His head is well separated from his front body or thorax, and he has two very long feelers which lie back over his body. His jaws are very strong, and if you give him a leaf to eat, under a glass, you can see how they move sideways to cut the food, and the upper and lower lips, through which he passes it to his chewing jaws inside.

If you have caught a female, she will have a curious long tube or egg-layer at the end of her body, which she forces into the ground, to lay her eggs, and this will show you the way that other smaller insects do it.

And now you will want to know how a grasshopper chirps, for you will remember that no insect can make any noise with its mouth. Put your finger gently along, under the left front wing of the great green Grasshopper, close to where it is joined to the body. You will feel that it is rough like a file. The grasshopper rubs this file against the edge of the other wing, and makes the rasping noise.

The small green Grasshopper, which has short feelers standing forward from his head, makes his chirping noise in another way. He has a file on the inside of his hind leg, which he rubs against the top of his wing. This little grasshopper is really a small locust, like those which fly in swarms over Europe, eating every green thing. which comes in their way. Fortunately for us, though he eats very greedily, our little friend is not so destructive as they are. Locusts have no egg laying tube; they drop their eggs into the loose earth and cover them up.

Crickets are very like grasshoppers, and make their chirping by rubbing their wings together. The females have long egg-laying tubes, as you will see if you can catch a mother cricket in the kitchen. She lays her eggs behind the oven or near the fireplace, where they will hatch all the year round in the warmth.

Grasshoppers and crickets do not chirp to please us, they are calling to each other. Therefore they must be able to hear. Where do you expect to find their ears? I am sure you will never guess.

Look under the wing of the small grasshopper on the first ring of his abdomen, the one behind his hind leg. There a little above his breathing holes, you will see a very small hole. This has a thin skin over it, and it is his ear. The great grasshopper has his ear in a still more curious place, on his front leg below his knee.

I expect you will know the Field-cricket, for though it is very timid, and seldom comes out in the day, yet if you find out where it lives, by its chirp, and poke a blade of grass down the cracks of the earth, it is sure to seize it, and you can draw it out. Many country children get them in this way. A Field-cricket is rather larger than the House-cricket; his body is more yellow, and his chirp much more shrill. He is very useful in the garden,

GREAT GREEN GRASSHOPPER'S LEG.
e. Ear.

for he feeds on insects as well as plants, sitting outside his hole at night to catch them. But by day he is always in the ground, where the young ones remain all the winter till they get their wings.

I wonder if you have ever found a Mole-cricket? There are plenty in England in sandy ground, especially in damp fields, and on the banks of canals and rivers. But they do not live in all parts of the country, and they are very shy. only coming out at night. They make a strange croaking cry, and by it you may know that there are some in your neighborhood. Then you must look along the river-bank, or in a sandy and damp part of

1. Great Green Grasshopper – Female with Egg Laying Tube.
2. Small Green Grasshopper.   3. Field Cricket.
4. Long-Winged Grasshoppers.   5. Wingless Female Grasshopper.

the garden, and if you can see ridges of earth thrown up, most likely the Mole-cricket will be working underneath.

He is a very curious insect, about half an inch long with a small head and long feelers, a very broad thorax, and thick flat front legs, ending in large feet like a mole, with sharp black claws. With these he digs his way through the earth, just as the mole does, and his body is covered with soft hairs, brown above, and yellow beneath, to keep off the damp earth. He

MOLE-CRICKET FLYING AND AT REST.

does great mischief if he gets into a garden, for he tunnels along, eating the roots and stems of the plants. The mother Mole-cricket has no egg-laying tube, for she does not want it underground. She lays about 200 eggs in a chamber at the end of the run, and the young Mole-crickets live there for two or three years before they get their wings. If you can find a nest, and get a few of the young ones, you may see their curious shape.

There are two other straight-winged insects which you

know quite well. One is the Earwig, of which some silly people are afraid, though it does no harm to anyone. Its pincers are used to fold its long hind wings under its short wing-cases, and the only mischief it does is to eat our flowers. The mother earwig is very affectionate. She carries away her eggs if they are disturbed, and watches over her little ones till they are full-grown.

The other straight-winged insect is the Cockroach, which people call "black beetle." It is not a beetle, for it does not grow out of a grub, and it is not black but brown. The young are like the old ones, only smaller and without wings. The mother cockroach never has any wings. She carries her eggs in a curious way at the end of her body in a case like a purse, and hides it behind the oven, or under the boards, just before the eggs are hatched. These cases are brown, horny, and shaped something like a bean. Inside there are about sixteen eggs, neatly arranged in two rows like peas in a pod. Cockroaches are very disagreeable and destructive insects. They eat everything they can get, and have a very repulsive smell.

Try to find the different kinds of grasshopper and cricket, both full grown and before they have their wings. Examine the wings of an earwig. Find the egg-cases of the cockroach.

LESSON XII.

ANTS AND THEIR HONEY-COWS.

ANTS are the most intelligent of all insects. We learnt a little about the home of the Hill-ant in Book I., to which you can look back for drawings of the male, female, and worker ants with their grubs and cocoons.

Now we will look at some other ants, and learn about their

ways. There are two very common kinds to be found in most gardens. One is red and the other black. They both build their homes underground, by clearing out the earth with their jaws and feet, and so making galleries and chambers. There is generally a little rise in the ground, where they are at work, making a dome above the nest, but it is not so conspicuous as the hill of the Hill-ant. If you dig a deep hole on one side of a nest you will open the chambers and see the grubs inside them, and, if you do not make it too big, the busy ants will soon put it right again.

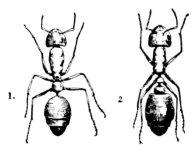

1. BLACK ANT WITH ONE KNOB IN THE WAIST.
2. RED AND WITH TWO KNOBS.

Then you will take a few cocoons, and put them in a little earth under a glass so as to see the young ants come out. But do not take the grubs, unless you take some grown-up ants with them, for they cannot feed themselves.

If you get a black and a red ant you will know them apart, not only by their colour, but because the black ant has one round knob in the thin part joining her hind body to her fore body, while the red ant has two knobs. By this we know that the red ant has a sting, and the black ant has none. All English ants which have two knobs to their abdomen can sting; but those with only one knob cannot (with one rare exception). These which have no sting attack their enemy with their strong jaws, and squirt out a strong acid over them.

There is a little yellow ant which lives in our houses and eats our food. She has two knobs, and stings quite sharply. I once cut open a cake which had been some days in the cupboard and found the middle full of these ants. They swarmed on my hand and made it tingle with their stings. This ant generally makes her home behind the fireplace.

If you put your ants under a glass, and give them a piece of nut or bread to eat, you may see them use their outer jaws to scrape the surface, and their tiny tongue to lick off the juice or oil, while they pass the food to the inner jaws, just as the bees and wasps did. You may also see them pause to stroke their body with their front legs. Look closely at these and you will see a small spur on a joint a little way up the leg. This spur has more than fifty fine teeth on it, and there are some coarse teeth on the leg itself. These are the ant's brush and comb. She scrapes herself with them, and then draws them through her outer jaws, or mandibles, to clean them.

She has very small eyes, and always uses her antennæ to find out anything she wants to know. These stand out in front of her curious flat head, and are very mysterious instruments. When ants want to talk to one another they touch their antennæ, and in some strange way they can tell each other where to go and what to do.

The Garden-ants live much more underground than the Hill-ants, but you may often see them sunning themselves in the garden, or cutting off blades of grass with their mandibles to line their nests, or tearing a spider or fly to pieces. They often seem to run hither and thither as if they did not know what they were doing, but if you watch you will find that each one has an object. Some are carrying things into the nest, others are climbing the stalks of the flowers to sip their honey. As these honey-laden ants go home, if they meet with an ant which has been doing other work and is hungry, the well-fed ant will squeeze honey out of her throat to feed her friend. For it seems to be a rule among ants that each one helps the other.

And now you must watch day by day till you see a much more wonderful thing. You will remember that we saw in the first lesson little plant-lice called Aphides sucking juice out of the stalks of plants. But we did not notice that they have two little horns at the end of their bodies. As they suck and suck they become too full, and the sweet juice often oozes out of these horns. You may see it standing in tiny drops on their tips.

This juice is just what the ant loves, and you may be fortunate enough to see the garden-ant take it, because she brings

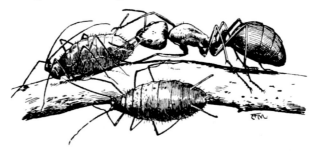

ANT TICKLING PLANT-LICE FOR HONEY.

the aphides and puts them on daisies near her nest. She goes up behind the aphis and strokes its sides with her antennæ, so that it gives out a drop of honey from its horns.

She has another herd of these honey-cows safely hidden underground where you cannot see them. She carries them down into her galleries, and puts them on the roots of plants. There she takes care of them, just as she does of her own grubs, and keeps their eggs and young ones through the winter, ready for the next spring. In our climate ants sleep through the winter, but in warmer countries they remain awake and store up food.

When you are digging into the nest of a Garden-ant look very carefully at the roots you dig up, and you will most likely see some plant-lice on them. If you put them carefully back they will be none the worse, and the little ant will not have lost her honey-cows.

There is a small yellow ant called the Meadow-ant, which lives in great numbers on heaths and meadows, and has no sting. She keeps nearly all her honey-cows underground, putting them on the roots of the grass. Sometimes when you are ploughing up a field you may cut through one of these nests. If you do, stop a minute and watch the ants. Their first care will be for the ant-grubs and cocoons. But as soon as these are carried down you will see them fetching the little green plant-lice as carefully as if they were their own children.

The Hill-ants do not bring their cows home. They visit them on the plants, and many battles between the ants of two nests begin because one colony has interfered with the other's cows. Then the working ants turn out of both nests and fall upon each other two and two, biting with their mandibles and standing on their hind legs, each trying to squirt formic acid over its enemy. These battles often go on for some days till one party is exhausted.

The battles are fought, and the honey-cows are milked, by the working ants, of which there may be thousands in a large nest. The queen-ants do no work, beyond laying the eggs. There may be two or three queen-ants in a large nest, and they never quarrel like queen-bees. When they are laying eggs in the home they have no wings. But in the summer there will be a number of winged male and female ants growing up in the nest, and some warm day they fly out, and you may see them rising and falling in the air like gnats. Then they tumble helplessly to the ground and crawl about. The males are eaten by birds or die. None of them go back to the nest. Those of the females which are not killed have their wings pulled off by the workers, or pull them off themselves, and they go back to lay eggs, or join a new nest.

Find any ants you can. Keep them a little, feeding them with honey and giving them some earth to build. Keep a few aphides on a plant to see the honey-drops. Examine an ant's nest by opening the side; put the aphides and cocoons back carefully.

Scientific Names of the Orders of Insects, with Explanation.

("-ptera" means wings.)

A-ptera .... *Without wings.* Fleas and Lice.

Hemi-ptera .... *Half-winged* – that is, wings horning in front, and transparent at the back. Plant-bugs, Aphides, frog-hoppers, and Water-boatmen.

Di-ptera .... *Two-winged.* Flies, Gnats, and Daddy-long-legs.

Lepido-ptera .. *Scale-winged.* The wings covered with fine scales. Butterflies and Moths.

Coleo-ptera ... *Sheath-winged.* The front wings horny, forming wing-cases. Beetles.

Neuro-ptera .. *Nerve-winged.* Wings covered with a network of nerves. Dragon-fly and May-fly.

Ortho-ptera .. *Straight-winged.* Wings folded in straight folds like a fan. Earwigs, Cockroach, Grasshopper, Locust, and Cricket.

Hymeno-ptera . *Membrane-winged.* Wings of transparent membrane. Bees, Wasps, Sand-wasps, Saw-flies, and Ants.

Made in the USA
Columbia, SC
12 August 2023